Grim, Gross and Grisly:

Disgusting facts about people

by

Anne Rooney

Illustrated by Mike Phillips

Check out Anne Rooney's website:
www.annerooney.co.uk

Or follow her on Twitter:
@annerooney

First published in 2010 in Great Britain by
Barrington Stoke Ltd
18 Walker St, Edinburgh, EH3 7LP

www.barringtonstoke.co.uk

ISBN: 978-1-84299-831-1

Printed in Great Britain by Bell & Bain Ltd

Contents

It's all about you

The human body is a wonderful thing. Your skin keeps your bits inside, and your bones and muscles keep you upright and let you move around. At least, when things are going well, that's how it works. But your body is also home to millions of germs and bugs, and can get some truly disgusting illnesses. This is not just other people we're talking about – it's you, too. Yes, you are as disgusting as everyone else.

Danger!

Some people treat their bodies like a playground or a science lab. They do some weird and wacky things. You should NOT try any of the things you read about in this book. Some of the people who did these things are dead – and with good reason (not just because they lived hundreds of years ago). And talking of being dead ... humans have done some pretty gross things with dead bodies over the years.

You might feel sick while you read this book – some of it is not very nice. And did you know that when you're sick, the same muscles that move food through your gut work backwards to move it back out of your mouth?

Ready? Got your sick bucket? Turn the page to find out just how horrible the human body really is ...

Chapter 1
Yucky you

You might think you look rather good – and I'm sure you do – but there's still a lot of yuck going on inside your body.

Goo and gunge

Your body makes all kinds of nasty slime and sludge.

Ear wax is made in your ears from a gluey yellow-brown stuff. Then it traps lots of dead skin, dirt, old germs and bits of dust.

Nice! Talking and chewing help to move the ear wax to the outside of your ear.

It's snot very nice to think about snot – or to pull it out with your finger. The slime in your nose dries and clumps into snot, but first it collects all the bits and pieces from the air you breathe in. Snot is full of dirt, dust, germs and pollen. It even includes tiny bits of asteroids – rocks from space!

Sweat doesn't smell on its own. Sweaty armpits and feet smell because germs are munching away on the sweat and making smelly chemicals – it's a bit like germ poo.

You make about a litre of spit each day. It starts to break down your food before you swallow it, and of course it helps you lick stamps and spit at your brother or sister.

One of the chemicals in bad breath is also made by dead bodies as they rot.

Body numbers

Do you like maths? Good – you're full of numbers ...

Your gut is all stuffed up inside you, which is just as well – by the time you're fully grown, it may be 9 m long.

You have one litre of blood for every 16 kg of body weight – so if you weigh 50 kg, that's about four juice-cartons full of blood.

Your stomach lining replaces itself every three days. The dead bits are digested along with the food you eat or come out in your poo.

Blood travels around your body in little tubes and if you could lay them end to end, they would go round the world two and a half times.

An adult human has about 2.5 kg of skin. If you could spread it out, it would be the size of a blanket. Just the right size to keep you warm.

Every square centimetre of your body has five million germs on it.

You have as many hairs as a chimpanzee – it's just that your hairs are much thinner so you don't look hairy.

The lungs are the only organ in your body that would float in water. If you could spread out your lungs so they were flat, they'd cover half a football pitch.

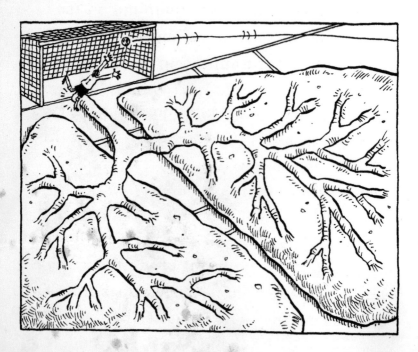

Solid bone is harder to break than concrete and twice as strong as steel. Problem is, your bones aren't solid, so they can break. Your bones are like a hard sponge – or an Aero bar – full of tiny holes. This makes them light. If your bones were solid, they would be too heavy to drag around!

Food, in and out

Your food may be very yummy on the way in – but nasty things happen to it inside you and it's not so appealing on the way out.

Don't pretend it wasn't you ... everybody farts. Quite a lot, in fact – about half a litre of gas a day. If you live 80 years, that's 14,600 litres of fart.

Farts come from air you have swallowed and gas made as your gut breaks down food. Even dead people fart – gas escapes from the gut after death.

If you fart in a lift, people can smell it for a long time – but not forever. Eventually, the fart particles fall to the floor or stick to the walls.

Fresh pee doesn't have germs in it. In old times, people used it to clean things, and even to wash their hair.

If you eat too much red beetroot, your pee turns pink!

You will pass 45,000 litres of pee in your life – enough to fill a small swimming pool.

Over your life-time, your gut will work through about 50 tons of food, turning a third of it into poo.

Poo is two thirds food waste, and one third dead germs, and bits of your insides that are not needed any more – dead cells from the inside of your gut.

Slugs and snails and puppy dogs' tails?

What are you made of? Well, there's the skin and bone and blood and muscle. But what are those made of? You'd be surprised!

You have lots of kinds of metal in your body. There's enough iron in you to make a nail. What size nail? Well, a small one when you're small and a bigger one, about 7 cm long, when you're grown up.

An adult has 206 bones, but a baby has about 300. This makes babies extra bendy (which is useful when you are being born). Some of the small bones grow together into larger bones as the child grows older.

There's one bone babies don't have, though – babies don't have knee-caps. At birth, the knee-cap is made of something called cartilage – a tough kind of body tissue that's not hard. It slowly turns to bone over a few years.

When you're fully grown, your body will contain enough of a mineral called sulphur to kill all the fleas on a medium-sized dog.

A normal-sized adult has enough body fat to make seven bars of soap. Human soap – yuck.

If you took out all the water from a grown-up there would be enough to fill four or five watering cans. And there would be a dried-up angry grown-up.

There is enough carbon in a human body to make 900 pencils. Which would you rather have – your dad or 900 pencils?

A person who weighs 70 kg contains 0.01 g of gold.

The bit at the end of a match is made out of something called phosphorous (say 'fos-for-us'). An adult contains enough phosphorous to make over 2,000 matches. It's stuck inside other chemicals in the body – so grown-ups don't burst into flames if you strike them.

You contain small amounts of other chemicals that are poisonous such as lead and chlorine.

An adult contains about 0.1 g of sodium and a bit more potassium. If you dropped this into water it would explode – luckily, it doesn't do that inside you so it's safe to have a bath.

Many of the chemicals in your body were made in stars at the start of the universe.

All the water you drink was once drunk by dinosaurs, and all the chemicals in your body were once in someone long dead. We are all made of recycled chemicals.

The chemicals in a human body are worth about £5.

Chapter 2

When it all goes horribly wrong ...

Being ill can be a lot worse than just feeling sick and having a snotty nose. There are some illnesses you really don't want to get, even to get off school. And the path to getting better can be just as bad.

Don't look now

Some illnesses are so horrible it will make you feel sick just to think about them.

The flesh-eating bug is very gross. It starts with a small cut that turns nasty and swells. Then you get a purple rash, and then small, round blisters full of dark liquid. You start to rot, and your skin splits open. It hurts – a lot. Later it goes numb, and your body starts to shut down. You can't breathe and bits of you turn black and drop off. That's never a good sign.

Another one to avoid is Ebola fever. It's easy to avoid because it's rare. First the fever, then the upset tummy, then the bleeding – from eyes, ears, nose, mouth and bottom. Slowly your insides turn to liquid and leak out of you until you die. Yuck.

If you have the illness called Ondine's curse you need a good memory, as you have to remember to breathe. If you forget, you die.

Eating your mum and dad after they die can make you mad – and dead. People who lived in New Guinea suffered a terrible illness called 'kuru'. It started with headaches, joint pain and shaking, and ended in death. A doctor found it was caused by people eating dead bodies at a feast held at funerals. The bit they liked most was the brain, and that was the most dangerous. They should have had crisps and sandwiches.

An illness called porphyria (say por-fee-re-a) may explain some stories about vampires. Victims turn very white, they are afraid of daylight and their teeth seem to grow longer as their gums shrink. Their teeth and finger-nails sometimes turn red, too.

Even a bad case of flu can kill you. In 1918 a very nasty flu spread around the world and killed 50–100 million people. Those who died were often healthy young people – but their bodies went too far in trying to fight the flu. Many drowned in their own blood as their lungs were eaten away.

People with the eating problem called pica eat anything at all. They can die from eating things that are sharp, dirty or poisonous – including broken bottles, paint, poo and stones. Some even eat parts of their own body.

Animals to the rescue

We've tried all kinds of strange things to help treat illness – but some of the strangest treatments use animals.

For years, people thought getting rid of extra blood would make sick people better. They often did this by letting leeches suck blood from them. A leech looks a bit like a black slug that lives in water – but think 'vampire slug', not garden slime-bag. The leech will suck blood until it is full and then drop off. Leeches are being used again – their spit thins the blood, helping people with some blood problems.

Nasty cuts can go bad if they get dirty. Luckily, maggots can eat the dead flesh and clean up wounds. (They don't eat healthy flesh, so there's no danger of them getting greedy and taking off a working arm or leg.) That's useful if you're left on a battlefield for days with a horrible wound and flies lay their eggs in it. Some hospitals use maggots to clean wounds.

Hundreds of years ago, Indian doctors used ants to stitch cuts. The doctor would hold the edges of the cut together and annoy an ant until it bit through the skin. Then they snapped off the ant's body, leaving its head holding the cut closed.

A dose of hookworm – a worm that lives in the gut – can cure hayfever and asthma. Hookworm dig through the skin and travel to the gut where they suck blood. Some people swallow hookworms on purpose to cure themselves of breathing problems.

Mind games

It's all in your mind – no, it really is – you are not a werewolf or a dead body. But there are illnesses that can make you think you are.

People with Cotard Syndrome (say 'sin-drome') believe they are the 'walking dead' – a dead body that can still walk around even when it's rotting. Some demand to be buried, and one woman got into a coffin and lay there until she really did die.

People with Diogenes Syndrome (say 'die-o-jen-ees') stop taking care of themselves. They get ill and smelly. They often keep rubbish and may fill their house with useless things. Some even have to make tunnels through the rubbish. No, you don't have it – you're just messy.

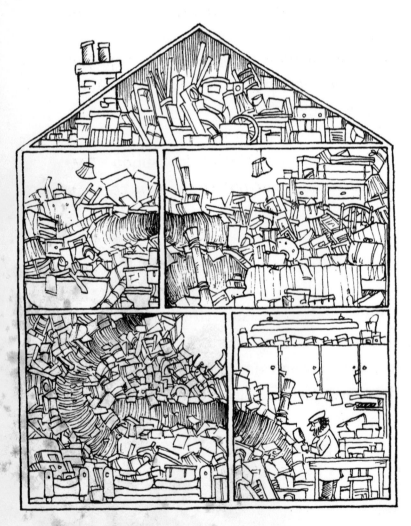

People with an illness known as BIID (the letters stand for Body Integrity Identity Disorder) want to cut off healthy parts of their body – some go so far as to cut off their fingers or even arms or legs.

Lycanthropes (say 'lie-can-throps') are people who believe they are werewolves. Well, perhaps they are.

The mental condition known as TTM makes people pull out their own hair – even their eyebrows and eyelashes – and sometimes eat it. That can cause a bit of a blockage in the gut, as well as baldness.

A horrible illness called windigo psychosis (say 'sie-co-sis') makes people really want to eat human flesh – but at the same time they're scared of becoming cannibals, so life's hard for them either way.

Chapter 3
Pesky pets

The animals we live with aren't all fluffy and sweet. You have more animals living in and on you than you want to know about. These animals are called parasites and they don't make nice pets – they eat you, or your food, or bits that drop off you.

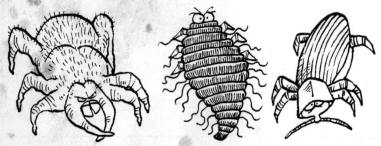

You're never alone

Think you sleep alone? Wrong! There are plenty of little animals crawling around your bed and your body every night.

"Sleep tight: don't let the bed bugs bite!" Bed bugs are tiny bugs that live in beds and sofas and soft chairs. They feast on human blood, often at night. They stab a small spike into your skin, then they suck your blood for up to fifteen minutes.

There are about a million mites and other bugs in your bed that live on all the bits that fall off you in the night.

House dust mites live all around us and feed on the flakes of dead skin that we shed all the time. You lose 1.5 g of skin each day – enough to feed a million house dust mites!

There are lots of special mites and bugs that have got used to living in or on different parts of human bodies. There are even bugs that live in the tiny holes where your eyelashes grow.

Bacteria are very tiny living things that can only be seen with a microscope. You have about 100 billion bacteria just on your skin, and plenty more living inside you. Some cause diseases, but others are really rather useful and help our bodies to work, breaking down food and sorting out waste for us.

Worms and other wigglers

Worms get everywhere – even inside you.

You can get worms that live in your gut if you eat their eggs in under-cooked food or in dirty water. People have even got worms from eating strips of dried meat from a mountain lion, or raw polar bear!

One type of worm lives just under the skin. You can watch it move around at the rate of about 1 cm an hour – yuck.

A tape-worm lives in your gut and eats whatever it likes of the food you eat. That means less of your food goes to making you fat – perfect if you want to lose weight.

The longest known tape-worm found inside a human was 11 m long. It was taken from an American woman in 1991 – she said

she was "really filled with joy" to know she
had the record tape-worm.

Screw worms are a type of maggot. The
fly lays about 200 eggs on a wound, or in
someone's nose or eye. The maggots hatch
and start munching away, eating the victim
from the inside out.

Small worms known as Guinea worms live
in the wall of the gut. After a year, the
females travel down to the feet and make a
little hole so that they can escape from the

body and lay eggs in pools of water. If the victim wants to get rid of the worm – and who wouldn't? – they have to find a doctor as soon as the worm appears. As the worm starts to come out of the hole, the doctor slowly winds it around a stick over several weeks.

What's eating you?

Some nasty beasties live in or on us just as a home, but others even eat us.

Head lice look like tiny beetles and live on your head. They suck your blood and make you itch, then lay eggs (nits) that hatch into even more head lice.

If you have a cat or dog, you might get flea bites sometimes. Fleas fall off your pet and jump from the floor onto you. They can't jump far, so most bites will be on your legs. Fleas suck your blood and leave an itchy spot.

Tiny mites burrow under the skin and cause a skin problem called scabies. The mites leave curly tunnels that look like white lines. It makes you itch like mad!

Remember those black slug-like leeches that doctors used to suck blood from sick people? If you take a dip in a river or pond, you might be attacked by a wild leech. Leeches stick to your skin, make a hole and suck your blood. Up close, a leech has a horrific-looking mouth with rows and rows of tiny teeth that let it clamp on. It's almost impossible to pull a leech off – best to leave it until it's full and lets go.

Mini monsters

Mini monsters living inside you can cause some horrible illnesses – it really is a case of 'better out than in'.

Some fleas can sick up bugs into your blood, too. They caused the Black Death plague which killed nearly half the people in Europe in the Middle Ages. Victims had horrific black boils, fever and terrible pain.

Mosquitoes don't live on you – they visit for a quick snack of yummy blood. But some mosquitoes carry tiny bugs inside them which they sick up into someone's blood.

These live and grow in the body and cause the deadly disease malaria.

A tiny bug that lives in the walls of mud houses in hot places such as South America causes something called Chagas disease. If it gets into your gut, it can stop you doing a poo. Waste builds up inside, leading to a horrible, slow death.

Sometimes people get a rare parasite and doctors have a hard time working out what's wrong with them. One woman complained she saw rainbows in sunny weather. It turned out she had parasites living inside her eyes.

Chapter 4
It takes all sorts ...

We're not all the same – and some of us are very strange, or do very strange things.

That big?

People come in all shapes and sizes – no, really, ALL shapes and sizes.

A man called Wesley Pemberton in the USA has leg hair that is 16.5 cm long.

A woman from America called Lee Redmond didn't cut her finger-nails between 1979 and 2009. The nail on her right thumb was 90 cm long. Her nails were cut in 2009 after she was in a car crash.

One of the heaviest British people of all time was David Lambert. When he died in 1809, he weighed 330 kg. He was nearly 3 m round the middle. Lambert charged people money to look at him. When he died, part of his house had to be taken down to get his body out, and his coffin had wheels fitted because it was too heavy to carry.

Charles Osborne was very unlucky – he hiccupped for 68 years, from 1922 to 1990.

An Indian monk who lived in Madras had hair nearly 8 m long in 1949 – the longest hair recorded.

The longest beard is 5.33 m long. Its owner died in 1927, but the beard itself is kept in a museum in Washington, USA.

Louise Hollis from America grew her toe-nails so long that added together they came to 221 cm. Her husband said she had to choose between the toe-nails and him – she kept the nails and got rid of him.

Freaky!

Some people are born with strange bodies, and other people do odd things to make their bodies look strange.

Garry Turner from the UK has really stretchy skin – he can pull skin from his neck up over his mouth! (You can watch it on YouTube.)

Two people have tattoos covering more than 99% of their bodies. Tom Leppard from Scotland has leopard spots tattooed all over his body – black spots with a yellow background. A man called Lucky Rich from Australia has a single black tattoo covering his whole body and adds white patterns over the top. He did have coloured tattoos, but covered them over when he ran out of space.

Sometimes people grow horns from their head. It's very rare. An old man in China had a horn 10 cm long grow out of the back of his head over five years.

Other people have horns added using plastic surgery. To start with, tiny fake horns are fitted under the skin. The skin slowly grows to cover them. Then the horns are swapped for larger ones. The 'horns' slowly grow bigger and bigger as the person has larger and larger implants fitted.

A student in Germany has developed a system of Braille tattoos – raised tattoos made by putting lumps of metal or plastic under the skin so that blind people can feel them.

If you're afraid of losing your jewellery, you could keep it safe under your skin. A woman in New Zealand has a bracelet that looks like beads but is actually buried beneath her skin! She had the beads put into her arm through tiny cuts.

Many people through history have made scars to decorate their body. It's called scarification (say 'sca-ri-fi-kay-shun'). By making cuts or burns, they make a pattern or picture in scars. In some places, people rub ash, plants or soil into the wounds to make the scars different colours.

Elaine Davidson, born in Brazil, has all parts of her body pierced and decorated with jewellery. She had more than 6,000 body piercings by 2009. Her jewellery weighs more than 3 kg – as much as three cartons of juice.

Until 100 years ago, the Chinese used foot-binding to keep girls' feet small. Around the age of four, the girl had her toes broken and curved under the foot, then the foot was bound with bandages. She wore the bandages for her whole life so that her feet stayed tiny. It was very painful, and made it difficult to walk. But girls who did not bind their feet were thought ugly and found it hard to get a husband.

Don't try this at home!

Doing an experiment in the science lab at school is one thing – but some people have done crazy experiments on their own bodies.

Farts burn with a blue and yellow flame because they contain methane – the gas that burns in gas cookers and fires. Only one third of people make farts that can catch fire. Don't try burning your farts – it's dangerous and lots of people get hurt trying. It's so embarrassing at the hospital ...

A doctor studying the disease yellow fever wanted to find out if you could catch it from other people. So he drank the vomit sicked up by someone with the disease (yuck). He was lucky he didn't get yellow fever, as you can catch it from someone else.

Thousands of years ago, people used to drill holes in each other's heads to let out demons they thought caused headaches. Today, some people use a power drill to do the same. No demons have ever been seen leaving a head through a drilled hole.

A scientist from Italy called Spallanzani wanted to know how the gut works. He swallowed little bits of meat tied to a string and then pulled them back out after they'd been broken down a bit. He proved acid in the stomach helps us digest our food.

The man who invented the first camera to see inside a body had to try it on a man from a circus who swallowed swords because it used a long, straight tube. No untrained person could ever swallow it.

A soldier from Canada was shot in the stomach in 1822. The doctor let the wound heal with a hole so that he could take out bits of half-digested food to find out how the stomach works. He found out useful information, but it can't have been very nice for the soldier.

Another scientist from Italy (they like experiments) spent 30 years in a special chair to help him watch his weight. His name was Santorio Santorio. He wasn't on a diet – he weighed everything he ate and drank and all his waste. He found out his waste didn't weigh as much as his food, but he didn't put on lots of weight, so his body was using up the food somehow.

In many places, boys have to carry out a special – often nasty – task to become men. In a village in Brazil, they put on a glove full of stinging insects called bullet fire ants. These ants have the worst sting of any insect in the world, so it hurts – a lot. The boys have to wear the gloves and dance for between 10 and 30 minutes. One Native American group hung boys from hooks pushed through the skin of the chest.

Wouldn't it be better to stay a boy and not bother with being a man?

... or this

Other people do weird and not-so-wonderful things with their bodies just for fun. They have an odd idea of fun.

A Frenchman called Mr Mangetout (his name means Mr Eat-Everything in French)

eats – well, everything. He's eaten glass,
rubber and metal – and even cars, televisions
and a small plane. It took two years to eat
the plane, cut into small chunks. Bananas
and hard-boiled eggs make him sick, though.

The man called Lucky Rich, with all the
tattoos, juggles chainsaws, rides a unicycle
and swallows swords. It's a job – someone's
got to do it.

French artists have grown 'living skin' tattoos from their own skin and pig skin. The artists say their tattoo art can be planted on someone else by skin grafting, so the tattoo becomes part of the person who buys it.

Another French artist, called Orlan, uses her own body as her canvas. She is slowly changing herself by having plastic surgery. She copies different parts of the faces of beautiful paintings and sculptures.

Orlan is also planning to make a coat out of human skin. She takes cells of her own skin and from people with skin of different colours and grows more. She will put the grown skin together and sew them into a coat.

Chapter 5
Moving on

What's the worst that can happen? Well, the one thing you definitely can't recover from is death.

It comes to us all in the end ...

If your head is cut off, you might be able to see, hear and think for another 20 seconds.

Each year, about 76 people die playing Twister. The game itself isn't dangerous.

People can die if they get drunk and have a bad fall as they are playing it.

Monks in Japan have been known to kill themselves in a very strange way. It's the most extreme task a monk can carry out to show he doesn't care about his body. It also leaves a reminder of their struggle that might help other monks. They eat and drink special seeds and potions to dry their body and break down fat. Then they go to sit in a closed coffin with an air tube and a bell.

Each day, the monk rings the bell to show he is still alive. When he no longer rings the bell, the other monks take away the air tube. The dead monk has turned into a mummy – rather like an Egyptian mummy.

It's possible to think yourself to death. No, that's not an excuse to get out of homework. A man who took an overdose of his medicine was near death until doctors told him the tablets were not real medicine – they were sugar pills. Then he recovered.

There have been several cases of people bursting into flames for no known reason. Sometimes there is nothing left of them at all.

You can't take it with you

Your body's no good to you once you're dead. So does it matter what happens to it?

It can take hundreds of years for a body to rot away to just a skeleton – it all depends on where it's buried.

Teeth and nails sometimes seem to grow after death – they don't really, but the flesh shrinks and this makes them look longer.

At 'body farms' scientists put dead bodies in different places and watch how they rot. It helps solve crimes – by looking at the creepy crawlies in the body, police scientists can work out how long the body has been dead and where it has been.

Hundreds of years ago, doctors and scientists in India weren't allowed to cut up dead bodies because of their beliefs. To find out how the human body works, they would put a dead body in a basket and leave it in a river until it went squishy. Then they could poke the flesh off with a stick and see what was inside.

When doctors and scientists started to explore the body, they couldn't get enough bodies to cut up. Grave robbers stole dead bodies from graves or took bodies of criminals from the gallows where they had

been killed and sold them to doctors. Some even killed people just to sell the body!

I want my mummy!

The Egyptians were not the only people to make mummies from dead bodies.

Some groups in South America made mummies long before the Egyptians. 7,000 years ago, they took the insides out of a dead body, or removed the skin. Sometimes they put sticks in to help keep the body straight. Then they stuffed the skin with bits of plant, and sometimes covered it with a clay paste and painted it. A well-dressed mummy had a painted clay mask, a wig and sometimes a clay hat to keep the wig on.

If a body is left in some kinds of mud it shrivels up and becomes a 'bog body'. The skin looks like dark brown leather, but the bones crumble away.

Ancient Egyptians took the insides out of a dead body and put them in special jars. Then they packed the body with a special tar called natron to dry it out. They dried the insides, too. After 40 days, they packed the body with sawdust and leaves. Then they put oil on the body and wrapped it up in bandages to make a mummy. In later times they put the dried insides back in the body with the sawdust.

A dried-out, frozen body found on a cold mountain-top in Austria in 1991 turned out to be 5,300 years old. At first, people thought the man had died recently because his skin and hair were in place. But he was a natural 'ice mummy'.

About 500–1000 years ago, the Inca people in South America made mummies which they wrapped in brightly coloured bundles, put in baskets or covered with large pots. Some had painted, staring eyes – spooky!

In Scotland, 3,500 years ago, people mummified their dead relatives and buried them under the floors of their houses. They kept the floor above the mummy clear.

Sometimes when a body is dug up it has not rotted at all. This happens because fat in the body turns into a kind of soap. The 'soap mummy' is pale and waxy looking. In the past, people often thought these bodies were saints or vampires.

There is a modern way of turning people and animals into mummies which is called Summum. The body is left in a tank of chemicals for a few months. The body stays looking natural and keeps so well that it might be possible to make clones (exact copies) from it some time in the future.

Getting rid of the evidence

There are lots of ways of getting rid of dead bodies besides just burying them or burning them.

In parts of Tibet and China, dead bodies are left out on the mountains for birds such as vultures to eat. This is called a 'sky burial'. It's pretty nasty – sometimes, relatives or monks cut the body into pieces and even smash the bones apart to help the birds to gobble up every last bit.

In eastern Russia, people left their dead to be eaten by dogs. They thought the person would be better off in the after-life if a dog ate their body.

Some tribes in Africa grind up the bones of their dead and sprinkle them on food.

The most expensive way of getting rid of a body is a 'space burial'. The dead body is first burnt and then some of the ashes are put in a tube and blasted into space in a rocket. The creator of the TV series *Star Trek* and the actor who played Scotty in the series both had space burials.

Some people have their body frozen after death. They hope that doctors will find a cure for what they died of and bring them back to life. Will people in the future want lots of old corpses brought back to life?

So were you sick? Were you surprised at how grim, gross and grisly your body is? We hope so!

AUTHOR CHECK LIST

Anne Rooney

What are your top three most disgusting facts about people which you couldn't fit in the book?

1. There are more cells in your body that are not you than that are you. Nine out of ten of the cells in your body belong to microbes and parasites living inside you!

2. In Ancient Egypt, people used to clean their teeth with a powder made of rock from volcanoes, burnt egg shells and ox hooves.

3. A few hundred years ago, people made a special medicine from a kind of green moss that only grows on human skulls. That is, the skulls of dead people – there isn't any moss in your head right now.

Which is your favourite fact in the book and why?

I love the thought that the water we drink was once drunk by dinosaurs – of course, it also means it once came out as dinosaur pee, which is not as nice.

What's the most sick you have ever been?

When I picked up what I thought was a bit of chocolate on the floor to eat it. It turned out to be a dried-out earthworm. Yuk!

ILLUSTRATOR CHECK LIST

Mike Phillips

Which is your favourite fact in the book and why?

That the longest beard is 5.33 m long.

My beard is less than 10 cm long.

What's the most sick you have ever been?

I was once very sea-sick on a hovercraft.

Would you rather wear a glove full of bullet fire ants or eat a plane bit by bit? And why?

I would rather eat anything bit by bit than go through the pain of bullet fire ants.

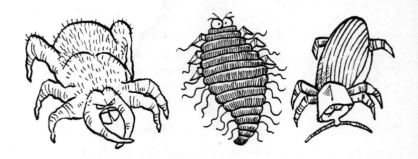

Barrington Stoke would like to thank all its readers for commenting on the manuscript before publication and in particular:

Carol Anthony
Rhys Arlow
Keisha Birrell
Karen Bradley
Ande Bray
Ainsley Chapman
Charlie
Caitlin Cotter Clarke
Jemma Cooper
Jamie Cunningham
James Docherty
Laura Dorrian
Shannon Dunn
Benita Fameyeh
Fergus Findlay
Nicole Forsyth
Di Frape

Kendal Gater
Lee Grant
Laura-Jane Harvey
Lorna Hodgetts
Oliver Jones
Chloe Kane
Christopher Russell
Wesley Lake
Catherine Lambillion-Jameson
Lewis Logie
Chloe Lowndes
Calum McConnachie
Deirdre McConnell
Rebecca McKernan
Lauren McRae
Marc Monaghan
Ryan Monteith

Lauryn Mutch
Shane Palfrey
Anne Palmer
Joseph Pettitt
Georgie Reilly
Robbie Reilly
Stephen Rodger
Jenny Rowlands
Karolina Rybak
Fatima Shah
Laaiba Shah
Denise Shortt
Steve Taylor
Joanne Tillman
Ryan Treece
Alex Turner
Cahya Umi
Jamie Ward

Become a Consultant!

Would you like to be a consultant? Ask your parent, carer or teacher to contact us at the email address below – we'd love to hear from them! They can also find out more by visiting our website.

schools@barringtonstoke.co.uk
www.barringtonstoke.co.uk